MORE UNCOMMON
PRAYERS

MORE UNCOMMON PRAYERS

An Anthology

by

CECIL HUNT

LONDON

HODDER AND STOUGHTON

First published August 1951
Second Impression 1955

PRINTED AND BOUND IN GREAT BRITAIN FOR HODDER AND STOUGHTON, LIMITED.
BY RICHARD CLAY AND COMPANY, LTD., BUNGAY, SUFFOLK.

AUTHOR'S PREFACE

MY first words must be of warmly sincere thanks to those who, from many countries, wrote in appreciation of my "Uncommon Prayers." Without their encouragement I should not have ventured upon this second anthology. With it, and the suggestions often made, it has been more easy, and, I trust, more helpful.

As some may come first to this later collection, I would repeat my earlier admission that I have no qualifications for compiling this book, beyond a love of literature and a belief that man is a trinity of body, mind and spirit; and that the godhead of that trinity must be the spirit. My hope is that it may be a help and a pleasure to some on the by-paths that lead to the Damascus Road.

I am conscious of omissions, although many of these are deliberate and others made necessary by the belief that such a book, to serve best its purpose, should be of handy size and modest price.

The incomparable collects of Cranmer and some of the best-loved hymns and prayers in the various collections of the churches are omitted. They are easy of pursuit. Some of the uncommon prayers here offered will be common to some readers; not all, I trust, to everyone. There are pages left at the end of the book whereon further favourites and discoveries may be written. For such a book should, to its advantage, assume a personal significance.

Many, myself included, never cease to be moved by the magnificence of our language in the hands of the masters; the more so when it clothes the highest aspirations in the hearts of men. Other prayers, less noble in their concept and texture, still present beautifully thoughts that are common to us all in our best moments. Sincerity has its inherent eloquence.

I think often of Cellini, the supreme Florentine goldsmith, who, in a turbulent life of mingled violence and exquisite integrity to the highest canons of his art, could write from the dungeon: " Mine eyes have seen God's glory without shield . . ."

If this book brings but a glimmer of beauty to some whose eyes are clouded and whose spirits are in desolation, I shall rest content in the fulfilment of its modest purpose. The literature of prayer is an inexhaustible library, and it is available to all. The questing spirit only is needed.

I thank sincerely those who have so kindly helped me with this book, and especially am I grateful to the Rev. John Birkbeck, Iran; B. C. Boulter, Rev. David Callum, J. S. Crockett, Ontario; Mrs. Margaret H. Hancock, Miss Teresa Hooley, Norman Hunt, Mrs. E. May Macnutt, Rev. Dr. Peter Marshall, Washington; Rev. Dr. Reinhold Niebuhr, Mass.; Sampson Low, Marston & Co., Ltd. (Donn Byrne); the executor of the late George MacDonald, Rev. F. D. Tyner, Minneapolis; Dr. Helen Waddell, Miss Mary Winter Were.

I do not think any copyright has been unwittingly infringed, but if it has it is not through lack of research, and any deficiencies will be gladly remedied in subsequent editions.

CECIL HUNT.

Great Dunmow,

Essex.

1951.

MORE UNCOMMON
PRAYERS

MANKIND can be, in fact, divided into three categories—those who find God and serve Him—those who, not having found Him as yet, are seeking for Him—and those who neither found nor yet seek.

The first are sensible and happy—the second sensible and unhappy—the last are unhappy and mad.

From " Pascal : The Man and the Message," by Roger H. Soltau, formerly Scholar of Pembroke College, Oxford.

So great a cloud of witnesses.—Hebrews xii. 1.

AND is there care in heaven? And is there love
In heavenly spirits to these creatures base
That may compassion of their evils move?
There is—or else more wretched were the case
Of men than beasts . . .

(The angels) for us fight, they watch and duly ward,
And their bright squadrons round about us plant;
And all for love, and nothing for reward:
O, why should Heavenly God to men have such regard!

Edmund Spenser, 1552–1599.

The sure relief of prayer.—WORDSWORTH.

BE not afraid to pray ; to pray is right.
Pray, if thou canst, with hope ; but ever pray,
Though hope be weak, or sick with long delay.
Pray in the darkness, if there be no light.
Far is the time, remote from human sight,
   When war and discord on the earth shall cease ;
   Yet every prayer for universal peace
   Avails the blessed time to expedite.

Whate'er is good to wish, ask that of Heaven,
Though it be what thou canst not hope to see :
Pray to be perfect, though material leaven,
Forbid the spirit so on earth to be ;
   But if for any wish thou dar'st not pray,
   Then pray to God to cast that wish away.

Ernest Hartley Coleridge, 1769–1849.

Mercy and truth be with thee.—II Samuel xv. 20.

From EXHORTATION TO PRAYER

HAVE you no words ! Ah, think again,
Words flow apace when you complain,
And fill your fellow-creature's ear
With the sad tale of all your care.

Were half the breath thus vainly spent,
To heaven in supplication sent ;
Your cheerful song would off'ner be,
" Hear what the Lord has done for me ! "

William Cowper, 1731–1800.

Speak, Lord ; for thy servant heareth.—I Samuel iii. 9.

THEY asked the abbot Macarius, saying, " How ought we to pray ? " and the old man said, " There is no need of much speaking in prayer, but often stretch out thy hands and say, ' Lord, as Thou wilt and as Thou knowest, have mercy upon me.' But if there is war in thy soul, add, ' Help me.' And because He knoweth what we have need of, He showeth us His mercy."

Dr. Helen Waddell, in " The Desert Fathers."

And they took knowledge of them, that they had been with Jesus.—Acts iv. 13.

OUR Father which in Heaven art,
   We sanctify Thy name ;
Thy Kingdom come, Thy will be done,
   In Heaven and Earth the same.
Give us this day, our daily bread,
   And us forgive Thou so,
As we on them that us offend,
   Forgiveness do bestow.
Into temptation lead us not,
   And us from evil free,
For Thine the Kingdom, Power and Praise
   Is and shall ever be.

George Wither, 1588–1667.

Thy will be done, though in my own undoing.—SIR THOMAS BROWNE.

From THE COMMON QUESTION

AND so I sometimes think our prayers
    Might well be merged in one;
And nest and perch and hearth and church
    Repeat " Thy will be done ! "

John Greenleaf Whittier, 1807–1892.

O heavy burden of a doubtful mind.—FRANCIS QUARLES.

THE saint, who walk'd on waves, securely trod
While he believ'd the beck'ning of his God.
But, when his faith no longer bore him out,
Began to sink, as he began to doubt.

John Dryden, 1631–1700.

Always in every prayer of mine for you all making request with joy.—Philippians i. 4.

From THE PRAYER SEEKER

HE prayeth best who leaves unguessed
The mystery of another's breast.
Why cheeks grow pale, why eyes o'erflow,
Or heads are white, thou need'st not know
Enough to note by many a sign
That every heart hath needs like thine.

Pray for us !

John Greenleaf Whittier, 1807–1892.

The prayers of Abel linked to deeds of Cain.—BYRON.

O LORD, the Lord whose ways are right, keep us in Thy mercy from lip-service and empty forms; from having a name that we live, but being dead.

Help us to worship Thee by righteous deeds and lives of holiness; that our prayer also may be set forth in Thy sight as the incense, and the lifting up of our hands be as an evening sacrifice.

Christina Rossetti, 1830–1894.

GOD, my Creator, stand by my side,
Keep Thou the door of my lips,
Guard Thou my hands,
O Lord of Light.

Accadian.

Thou shalt not harden thine heart, nor shut thine hand from thy poor brother.—Deuteronomy xv. 7.

From DIVINE COMPASSION

. . . Is heaven so high

That pity cannot breathe its air ?

Its happy eyes forever dry,

Its holy lips without a prayer !

My God ! My God ! if thither led

By Thy free grace unmerited,

No crown nor palm be mine, but let me keep

A heart that still can feel, and eyes that still can weep.

John Greenleaf Whittier, 1807–1892.

The trivial round, the common task,
Will furnish all we need to ask. . . .—JOHN KEBLE.

THE day returns and brings us the petty round of irritating concerns and duties. Help us to play the man, help us to perform them with laughter and kind faces. Let cheerfulness abound with industry. Give us to go blithely on our business all this day, bring us to our resting-beds weary and content and undishonoured, and grant us in the end the gift of sleep.

R. L. Stevenson, 1850–1894.

GRANT us, O Lord, to pass this day in gladness and in peace, without stumbling and without stain ; that, reaching the eventide victorious over all temptation, we may praise Thee, the eternal God, who art blessed, and dost govern all things, world without end.

Mozarabic.

The day-spring from on high.—Luke i. 78.

MY PRAYER

I THANK Thee, Lord, for Thy great gift,
    Another morn to see.
My prayer be this—that if I live
    The day be spent for Thee.

May I do naught to thwart Thy will,
    But seek in every way
To do what Thou would'st have me do
    Throughout the livelong day.

May I, when eventide arrives,
    Bring back the day to Thee?
Filled to the brim with deeds of love,
    Kindness and Charity.

My tasks well done—at eventide—
    I then can rest in peace,
Knowing that Thou wilt bless it all,
    I can from labour cease.

And when the Day of Life is done
    And Deathly Night doth fall,
If I can hear Thee say " Well Done,"
    Then sweet will be the call.

Margaret H. Hancock.

For thou knowest not what a day may bring forth.—
Proverbs xxvii. 1.

O LORD our God, who hast chased the slumber from our
eyes, accept our prayers and supplications, and give us faith
that maketh not ashamed, confident hope and love un-
feigned; bless our coming in and going out, our thoughts,
words and works, and grant us to begin, continue and end
this day with the praise of the unspeakable sweetness of Thy
mercy.

PRAISED be Thou, O God, who dost make the day bright
with Thy sunshine, and the night with the beams of
heavenly fires. Listen now to my prayers; watch over me
with Thy power; give me grace to pass all the days of my
life blamelessly, free from sin and terror. For with Thee is
mercy and plenteous redemption, O Lord, my God.

Greek Liturgy.

Acquaint now thyself with him, and be at peace.—Job xxii. 21.

MATINS; or, MORNING PRAYER

WHEN with the virgin morning thou dost rise,
Crossing thyself, come thus to sacrifice :
First wash thy heart in innocence, then bring
Pure hands, pure habits, pure, pure everything.
Next to the altar humbly kneel, and thence
Give up thy soul in clouds of frankincense.
Thy golden censers, filled with odours sweet,
Shall make thy actions with their ends to meet.

Robert Herrick, 1591–1674.

Purge your conscience from dead works to serve the living God.—Hebrews ix. 14.

I NEED Thee to teach me day by day, according to each day's opportunities and needs. Give me, O my Lord, that purity of conscience which alone can receive, which alone can improve Thy inspirations.

My ears are dull, so that I cannot hear Thy voice. My eyes are dim, so that I cannot see Thy tokens. Thou alone canst quicken my hearing, and purge my sight, and cleanse and renew my heart.

Teach me to sit at Thy feet, and to hear Thy word.

John Henry Newman, 1801–1890.

Consecrate yourselves today to the Lord.—Exodus xxxii. 29.

ETERNAL God, who committest to us the swift and solemn trust of life ; since we know not what a day may bring forth, but only that the hour for serving Thee is always present, may we wake to the instant claims of Thy holy will ; not waiting for tomorrow, but yielding today.

Lay to rest, by the persuasion of Thy spirit, the resistance of our passion, indolence or fear. Consecrate with Thy presence the way our feet may go ; and the humblest work will shine, and the roughest places be made plain.

Lift us above unrighteous anger and mistrust into faith and hope and charity by a simple and steadfast reliance on Thy sure will. In all things draw us to the mind of Christ, that Thy lost image may be traced again, and Thou mayest own us as at one with Him and Thee.

Dr. James Martineau, 1805–1900.

And he said, My presence shall go with thee, and I will give thee rest.—Exodus xxxiii. 14.

BLESSED art Thou, O Lord our God, the God of our fathers, who turnest the shadow of death into the morning; who hast lightened mine eyes that I sleep not in death.

O Lord, blot out as a night-mist mine iniquities. Scatter my sins as a morning cloud. Grant that I may become a child of the light, and of the day. Vouchsafe to keep me this day without sin. Uphold me when I am falling, and lift me up when I am down. Preserve this day from any evil of mine, and me from the evils of the day. Let this day add some knowledge, or good deed, to yesterday.

Oh, let me hear Thy loving-kindness in the morning, for in Thee is my trust. Teach me to do the thing that pleaseth Thee, for Thou art my God. Let Thy loving Spirit lead me forth into the land of righteousness.

Lancelot Andrewes, 1555–1626.

Come unto me, all ye that labour and are heavy laden, and I will give you rest.—Matthew xi. 28.

A HOUSEWIFE'S PRAYER

THE privilege of yielding unto Thee,
The day with all it holds in store for me,
In every act to do it as for Thee.
    A housewife's humble prayer.

To start the day with all its duties small
And claim Thy strength and promised help in all.
To know that Thou wilt answer ere I call.
    A housewife's answered prayer.

To offer unto Thee when night draws nigh
A humble worship—penitential sigh.
To have Thy Blessing as Thou passest by.
    A housewife's grateful prayer.

Margaret H. Hancock.

Behold, I have longed after thy precepts; quicken me in thy righteousness.—Psalm cxix. 40.

I KNOW, O Lord, and do with all humility acknowledge myself an object altogether unworthy of Thy love; but sure I am, Thou art an object altogether worthy of mine.

I am not good enough to serve Thee, but Thou hast a right to the best service I can pay.

Do Thou then impart to me some of that excellence, and that shall supply my own want of worth. Help me to cease from sin according to Thy will, that I may be capable of doing Thee service according to my duty.

Enable me so to guard and govern myself, so to begin and finish my course that, when the race of life is run, I may sleep in peace and rest in Thee.

Be with me unto the end, that my sleep may be rest indeed, my rest perfect security, and that security a blessed eternity.

St. Augustine, 354–430.

Full of compassion, and gracious ; long-suffering, and plenteous in mercy and truth.—Psalm lxxxvi. 15.

O GOD, though our sins be seven, though our sins be seventy times seven, though our sins be more in number than the hairs of our head, yet give us grace in loving penitence to cast ourselves down into the depths of Thy Compassion.

Christina Rossetti, 1830–1894.

SHE sat and wept, and with her untressed hair
Still wiped the feet she was so blest to touch ;
And He wiped off the soiling of despair
From her sweet soul—because she loved so much.

Dante Gabriel Rossetti, 1828–1882.

Why, seeing times are not hidden from the Almighty, do they that know him not see his days?—Job xxiv. 1.

LORD, I have prayed so long
" My will be done."
Yet Thou hast gentle been.
Thou hast not judged my wrong
But waited till I'd won
Thought more serene.

Alas ! O Lord, not yet
Can I lay claim
To find surrender dear.
Yet would I leave my fret
Or think of it with shame
Since Thou art near.

But, giving all, I learn
That nothing's lost
And only given so.
Then do Thou help me turn
And wish, whate'er the cost,
My Overthrow.

Norman Hunt.

A noble mind disdains not to repent.—POPE.

"JESUS, thou present Saviour! Thou hast known the depths of all sorrow : Thou hast entered that black darkness where God is not, and hast uttered the cry of the forsaken. Come, Lord, and gather of the fruits of Thy travail and Thy pleading : stretch forth Thy hand, Thou who art mighty to save the uttermost . . .,

"See Lord—I bring her, as they of old brought the sick and helpless, and Thou didst heal them. . . . Make her feel the presence of the living God, who beholds all the past, to whom darkness is as noonday ; who is waiting now, at the eleventh hour, for her to turn to Him. . . .

"Thou—Thou wilt breathe on the dead soul, and it shall arise from the unanswering sleep of death.

"Yea, Lord, I see Thee, coming through the darkness, coming, like the morning, with healing on Thy wings. The marks of Thy agony are upon Thee—I see, I see Thou art able and willing to save—Thou will not let her perish for ever.

"Come, mighty Saviour! let the dead hear Thy voice ; let the eyes of the blind be opened : let her see that God encompasses her ; let her tremble at nothing but at the sin that cuts her off from Him. Melt the hard heart ; unseal the closed lips : make her cry with her whole soul, ' Father, I have sinned. . . .' "

Dinah Morris, the Methodist, in the condemned cell of Hetty Sorrel, in " Adam Bede," by George Eliot (Mary Ann Cross, 1819–1880).

In the multitude of thy mercy hear me, in the truth of thy salvation.—Psalm lxix. 13.

O MERCIFUL God, full of compassion, long-suffering and of great pity, make me earnestly repent, and heartily to be sorry for all my misdoings ; make the remembrance of them so burdensome and painful that I may flee to Thee with a troubled spirit and a contrite heart ; and, O merciful Lord, visit, comfort, and relieve me ; excite in me true repentance ; give me in this world knowledge of Thy truth and confidence in Thy mercy, and, in the world to come, life everlasting.

Strengthen me against sin, and enable me so to perform every duty that whilst I live I may serve Thee in that state to which Thou hast called me ; and, at last, by a holy and happy death, be delivered from the struggles and sorrows of this life, and obtain eternal happiness, for the sake of our Lord and Saviour, Thy Son Jesus Christ.

Dr. Samuel Johnson, 1709–1784.

In chains . . . they shall make supplication unto thee.—
Isaiah xlv. 14.

O LORD my God. I have hoped in Thee,
O dear Jesus, set me free.
Though hard the chains that fasten me,
And sore my lot, yet I long for Thee
I languish and groaning bend my knee,
Adoring, imploring, O set me free.

Mary, Queen of Scots (1542–1587), on the eve of her execution.

Life is a long lesson in humility.—BARRIE.

TO HIS EVER-LOVING GOD

Can I not come to Thee, my God, for these
So very-many-meeting hindrances,
That slack my pace ; but yet not make me stay ?
Who slowly goes, rids (in the end) his way.
Clear Thou my paths, or shorten Thou my miles,
Remove the bars, or lift me o'er the stiles :
Since rough the way is, help me when I call,
And take me up ; or else prevent the fall.
I kenn my home ; and its affords some ease,
To see far off the smoking villages.
Fain would I rest ; yet covet not to die,
For fear of future-biting penury :
No, no, my God, Thou know'st my wishes be
To leave this life, not loving it, but Thee.

Robert Herrick, 1591–1674.

He who repents having sinned is almost innocent.—
SENECA.

" FATHER, we're all gone far away, we have spent all, we are poor, we are tired of it all ; we want to feel different, to be different. We want to come back. Jesus came to save us from our sins and He said if we came He wouldn't cast us out, no matter how bad we were, if only we came back to Him. Oh, Jesus Christ, we are a poor lot, and I'm the worst of the lot, and we are trying to find the way. Show us how to get back, Amen."

The camp renegade in " Black Rock," by Ralph Connor (Rev.
C. W. Gordon, 1860–1937).

Repentance is the May of the virtues.—Chinese proverb.

" Saviour of sinners ! when a poor woman, laden with sins, went out to the well to draw water, she found Thee sitting at the well. She knew Thee not ; she had not sought Thee ; her mind was dark ; her life was unholy. But Thou didst speak to her, Thou didst teach her, Thou didst show her that her life lay open before Thee, and yet Thou wast ready to give her that blessing which she had never sought.

" Jesus ! Thou art in the midst of us, and Thou knowest all men . . . if their minds are dark, their lives unholy— if they have come out not seeking Thee, not desiring to be taught ; deal with them according to the free mercy which Thou didst show to her. Speak to them, Lord ; open their ears to my message ; bring their sins to their minds, and make them thirst for that salvation which Thou art ready to give.

" Lord, Thou art with Thy people still ; they see Thee in the night-watches, and their hearts burn within them as Thou talkest with them by the way. And Thou art near to those who have not known Thee ; open their eyes that they may see Thee—see Thee weeping over them . . . see Thee saying, ' Father, forgive them, for they know not what they do '—see Thee as Thou wilt come again in Thy glory to judge them at the last."

The Methodist, Dinah Morris, in " Adam Bede," by George Eliot
(Mary Ann Cross, 1819–1880).

Conscience is the voice of the soul; the passions are the voice of the body.—ROUSSEAU.

O FATHER, calm the turbulence of our passions; quiet the throbbing of our hopes; repress the waywardness of our wills; direct the motions of our affections; and sanctify the varieties of our lot.

Be Thou all in all to us; and may all things earthly, while we bend them to our growth in grace, and to the work of blessing, dwell lightly in our hearts, so that we may readily, or even joyfully, give up whatever Thou dost ask for.

May we seek first Thy kingdom and righteousness; resting assured that then all things needful shall be added unto us.

Father, pardon our past ingratitude and disobedience; and purify us, whether by Thy gentler or Thy sterner dealings, till we have done Thy will on earth, and Thou removest us to Thine own presence with the redeemed in heaven.

Mary Carpenter, 1807–1887.

Esteeming the reproach of Christ greater riches than the treasures in Egypt.—Hebrews xi. 26.

TO GOD

Do with me, God! as Thou didst deal with John
(Who writ that heavenly Revelation);
Let me, like him, first cracks of thunder hear;
Then let the harp's enchantments strike the ear;
Here give me thorns; there, in thy kingdom, set
Upon my head the golden coronet;
There give me day; but here my dreadful night:
My sackcloth here; but there my stole of white.

Robert Herrick, 1591–1674.

I dwell . . . . with him that is of a contrite and humble spirit.—Isaiah lvii. 15.

From THE CONTRITE HEART

THE Lord will happiness divine
  On contrite hearts bestow ;
Then tell me, gracious God, is mine
  A contrite heart, or no ?

I hear, but seem to hear in vain,
  Insensible as steel ;
If ought is felt, 'tis only pain.
  To find I cannot feel.

Oh make this heart rejoice, or ache ;
  Decide this doubt for me ;
And if it be not broken, break,
  And heal it, if it be.

William Cowper, 1731–1800.

In singleness of your heart, as unto Christ.—Ephesians
vi. 5.

From THE HAPPY CHANGE

How blest thy creature is, O God,
    When with a single eye,
He views the lustre of thy Word,
    The day-spring from on high!

William Cowper, 1731–1800.

A man is justified by faith.—Romans iii. 28.

O MY Father, I have moments of deep unrest—moments when I know not what to ask by reason of the very excess of my wants. I have in these hours no words for Thee, no conscious prayers for Thee.

My cry seems purely worldly; I want only the wings of a dove that I may flee away. Yet all the time Thou hast accepted my unrest as a prayer. Thou hast interpreted its cry for a dove's wings as a cry for Thee, Thou hast received the nameless longings of my heart as the intercessions of Thy Spirit.

They are not yet the intercessions of my spirit; I know not what I ask. But Thou knowest what I ask, O my God. Thou knowest the name of that need which lies beneath my speechless groan. Thou knowest that, because I am made in Thine image, I can find rest only in what gives rest to Thee; therefore Thou hast counted my unrest unto me for righteousness, and hast called my groaning Thy Spirit's prayer.

Rev. George Matheson, 1842–1906.

Who shall separate us from the love of Christ?—Romans
viii. 35.

I SEEK to serve, dear Lord,
And thus to follow Thee ;
To walk in lowly ways,
In true humility.

I seek to heal, dear Lord,
I would not injure Thee ;
For man I cannot wound
Without first wounding Thee.

I seek to love, dear Lord,
I seek to follow Thee,
Thou who art wholly Love
Draw near, be Love in me.

Margaret H. Hancock.

Who will not suffer you to be tempted above that ye are able ; but will with the temptation also make a way to escape.—I Corinthians x. 13.

GIVE me, O Lord,
A steadfast heart, which no unworthy affection may drag
   downwards ;
Give me an unconquered heart, which no tribulation can
   wear out ;
Give me an upright heart, which no unworthy purpose may
   tempt aside.

St. Thomas Aquinas, c. 1225–1274.

O GOD, by Thy mercy strengthen us who lie exposed to the rough storms of troubles and temptations. Help us against our own negligence and cowardice, and defend us from the treachery of our unfaithful hearts. Succour us, we beseech Thee, and bring us to Thy safe haven of peace and felicity.

St. Augustine, 354–430.

What God hath cleansed, that call not thou common.— Acts x. 15.

O GOD, Thou art Life, Wisdom, Truth, Bounty, and Blessedness, the Eternal, the only true Good. My God and my Lord, Thou art my hope and my heart's joy.

I confess, with thanksgiving, that Thou hast made me in Thine image, that I may direct all my thoughts to Thee, and love Thee.

Lord, make me to know Thee aright, that I may more and more love, enjoy, and possess Thee. And since, in the life here below, I cannot fully attain this blessedness, let it at least grow in me day by day, until it all be fulfilled at last in the life to come.

Here be the knowledge of Thee increased, and there let it be perfected. Here let my love to Thee grow, and there let it ripen; that my joy being here great in hope, may there in fruition be made perfect.

St. Anselm, 1033–1109.

If we live in the Spirit, let us also walk in the Spirit.—
Galatians v. 25.

O MOST merciful Redeemer,
Friend and Brother,
May we know Thee more clearly,
Love Thee more dearly,
And follow Thee more nearly;
For Thine own sake.

Richard of Chichester, fourteenth century.

O LORD, grant all who contend for the faith, never to
injure it by clamor and impatience; but, speaking Thy
precious truth in love, so to present it that it may be
loved, and that men may see in it Thy goodness and
beauty.

William Bright, 1824–1901.

A vain shadow strikes the anxious with fear.—OVID.

MOST loving Father, who hast taught us to dread nothing save the loss of Thee, preserve me from faithless fears and worldly anxieties, from corrupting passions and unhallowed love of earthly treasures ; and grant that no clouds of this mortal life may hide me from the light of that love which is immortal and which Thou hast manifested unto us in Thy Son, Jesus Christ our Lord.

William Bright, 1824–1901.

Fear God, and keep his commandments : for this is the whole duty of man.—Ecclesiastes xii. 13.

TEACH me, O Lord, and enable me to live the life of saints and angels. Take me out of the languor, the irritability, the sensitiveness, the anarchy, in which my soul lies, and fill it with Thy fulness.

Breathe on me with that Breath which infuses energy and kindles fervour. In asking for fervour, I ask for all that I can need, and all that Thou canst give. In asking for fervour, I am asking for faith, hope, and charity, in their most heavenly exercise ; I am asking for that loyal perception of duty which follows on yearning affection ; I am asking for sanctity, peace, and joy, all at once. Nothing would be a trouble to me, nothing a difficulty, had I but fervour of soul.

Lord, in asking for fervour, I am asking for Thyself, for nothing short of Thee, O my God. Enter my heart, and fill it with fervour by filling it with Thee.

John Henry Newman, 1801–1890.

And that ye study to be quiet, and to do your own business.—I Thessalonians iv. 11.

AGAINST INQUISITIVE AND PERPLEXING THOUGHTS

O LORD, my Maker and Protector, who hast graciously sent me into this world to work out my salvation, enable me to drive from me all such unquiet and perplexing thoughts as may mislead or hinder me in the practice of those duties which Thou hast required.

When I behold the works of thy hands, and consider the course of thy providence, give me grace always to remember that thy thoughts are not my thoughts, nor thy ways my ways.

And while it shall please thee to continue me in this world, where much is to be done, and little to be known, teach me by thy Holy Spirit, to withdraw my mind from unprofitable and dangerous enquiries, from difficulties vainly curious, and doubts impossible to be solved.

Let me rejoice in the light which Thou hast imparted, let me serve Thee with active zeal and humble confidence, and wait with patient expectation for the time in which the soul which Thou receivest shall be satisfied with knowledge. Grant this, O Lord, for Jesus Christ's sake.

Dr. Samuel Johnson, 1709–1784.

GRANT me, I beseech Thee, Almighty and most Merciful God, fervently to desire, wisely to search out, and perfectly to fulfil all that is well-pleasing unto Thee.

Order Thou my worldly condition to the glory of Thy name; and, of all that Thou requirest me to do, grant me the knowledge, the desire and the ability, that I may so fulfil it as I ought, and may my path to Thee, I pray, be safe, straightforward and perfect to the end.

Give me, O Lord, a steadfast heart, which no unworthy affection may drag downwards; give me an unconquered heart, which no tribulation can wear out; give me an upright heart, which no unworthy purpose may tempt aside.

Bestow upon me also, O Lord my God, understanding to know Thee, diligence to seek Thee, wisdom to find Thee, and a faithfulness that may finally embrace Thee.

St. Thomas Aquinas, c. 1225–1274.

That was the true Light, which lighteth every man that cometh into the world.—John i. 9.

GIVE me, O Lord, purity of lips, a clean and innocent heart; humility, fortitude, patience.

Give me the Spirit of wisdom and understanding, the Spirit of counsel and strength, the Spirit of knowledge and godliness, and of Thy fear.

Make me ever to seek Thy face with all my heart, all my soul, all my mind; grant me to have a contrite and humble heart in Thy Presence.

Most high, eternal and ineffable Wisdom, drive away from me the darkness of blindness and ignorance; most high and eternal Strength, deliver me; most high and eternal Light, illuminate me; most high and infinite Mercy, have mercy on me.

Gallican Liturgy, ninth century.

A generous prayer is never presented in vain.—R. L. STEVENSON.

O DIVINE Master, grant that I may not so much seek
To be consoled, as to console ;
To be understood, as to understand ;
To be loved, as to love ;
For it is in giving that we receive,
It is in pardoning that we are pardoned,
And it is in dying that we are born
To Eternal Life.

St. Francis of Assisi, 1182–1226.

For the obedience of faith.—Romans xvi. 26.

O GOD, who hast commanded us to be perfect, as Thou art perfect; put into my heart, I pray Thee, a continual desire to obey Thy holy will. Teach me day by day what Thou wouldst have me to do, and give me grace and power to fulfil the same. May I never from love of ease, decline the path which Thou pointest out, nor, for fear of shame, turn away from it.

Henry Alford, 1810–1871.

GOD grant me the serenity
To accept the things I cannot change,
The courage to change the things I can,
And the wisdom to know the difference.

Rev. Dr. Reinhold Niebuhr.

He giveth grace unto the lowly.—Proverbs iii. 34.

Thou O Christ art all I want,
More than all in Thee I find.
Raise the fallen, cheer the faint,
Heal the sick, and lead the blind.
Just and holy is Thy name
I am all unrighteousness
Vile and full of sin I am
Thou art full of truth and grace.

Plenteous grace with Thee is found,
Grace to cover all my sin.
Let the healing streams abound,
Make and keep me pure within.
Thou of life the fountain art,
Freely let me take of Thee ;
Spring Thou up within my heart,
Rise to all eternity.

Charles Wesley, 1707–1788.

THE CELESTIAL SURGEON

IF I have faltered more or less
In my great task of happiness;
If I have moved among my race
And shown no glorious morning face;
If beams from happy human eyes
Have moved me not; if morning skies,
Books, and my food, and summer rain
Knocked on my sullen heart in vain:
Lord, thy most pointed pleasure take
And stab my spirit broad awake;
Or, Lord, if too obdurate I,
Choose thou, before that spirit die,
A piercing pain, a killing sin,
And to my dead heart run them in!

R. L. Stevenson, 1850–1894.

O HOLY Spirit, Love of God, powerful Advocate and sweetest Comforter, infuse Thy grace and descend plentifully into my heart, for in whomsoever Thou dwellest, the Father and the Son come likewise and inhabit that breast. O come, Thou Cleanser of all inward pollutions, and Healer of spiritual wound and diseases. Come, in much mercy, and make me fit to receive Thee.

St. Augustine, 354–430.

For I reckon that the sufferings of this present time are not worthy to be compared with the glory which shall be revealed in us.—Romans viii. 18.

SWEET is e'en sorrow, coming in His name,
    Nor will I seek its purpose to explore,
His praise will I continually proclaim,
    And bless him evermore.

Abraham ibn Ezra, 1092–1167.

In your patience possess ye your souls.—Luke xxi. 19.

LORD, abate my great affliction, or increase my patience;
but, Lord, I repine not, I am dumb, Lord, before Thee,
because Thou doest it.

and

THAT, through these Labyrinths, not my groveling Wit,
But thy Silk-twist, let down from Heaven to me;
Did both conduct, and teach me, how by it,
                    To climb to thee.

George Herbert, 1593–1633.

Perfect through sufferings.—Hebrews ii. 10.

ALMIGHTY and most merciful Father, whose loving kindness is over all Thy works, behold, visit, and relieve this
Thy servant, who is grieved with sickness. Grant that the
sense of her weakness may add strength to her faith, and
seriousness to her repentance. And grant that by the help
of Thy Holy Spirit, after the pains and labours of this short
life, we may all obtain everlasting happiness, through Jesus
Christ our Lord, for whose sake hear our prayers.

Dr. Samuel Johnson, 1709–1784, at the death-bed of a friend.

For thine is the kingdom, and the power, and the glory.—
Matthew vi. 13.

BRING us, O Lord God, at our last awakening into the
house and gate of heaven, to enter into that gate and dwell
in that house, where there shall be no darkness nor dazzling,
but one equal light; no noise nor silence, but one equal
music; no fears nor hopes, but one equal possession; no
ends nor beginnings, but one equal eternity; in the
habitations of Thy glory and dominion world without end.

John Donne, 1572–1631.

. . . for I also had my hour; One far fierce hour and sweet.—G. K. CHESTERTON.

O GOD, you have called me and I come. I have spoken with the voice which you gave me. I have written with the words which you taught me.

So I pass along the road like an over-laden donkey, with hanging head. I am ready to go wherever and whenever you wish. The Angelus is ringing.

B. C. Boulter, from the French of Francis Jammes.

The souls of the righteous are in the hands of God.—
Wisdom iii. 1.

ALMIGHTY, eternal God, to whom there is never any
prayer made without hope of mercy, be merciful to the
souls of Thy servants departed from this world in the
confession of Thy name, that they may be associated to the
company of Thy saints.

Queen Elizabeth (1558–1603), Prayer for All Souls.

For the Lord shall be thine everlasting light, and the days of thy mourning shall be ended.—Isaiah lx. 20.

VESTA

O CHRIST of God! whose life and death
    Our own have reconciled,
Most quietly, most tenderly
    Take home Thy star-named child!

Thy grace is in her patient eyes,
    Thy words are on her tongue;
The very silence round her seems
    As if the angels sung.

Her smile is as a listening child's
    Who hears its mother call;
The lilies of Thy perfect peace
    About her pillow fall.

She leans from out our clinging arms
    To rest herself in Thine;
Alone to Thee, dear Lord, can we
    Our well-beloved resign!

Oh, less for her than for ourselves
    We bow our heads and pray;
Her setting star, like Bethlehem's,
    To Thee shall point the way!

John Greenleaf Whittier, 1807–1892.

The hand of God hath touched me.—Job xix. 21.

IN MANUS TUAS

INTO thy hands, Almighty Father, who dost will peace and purpose loving-kindness, we commend our spirits : our minds to know thee, our hearts to love thee, our wills to serve thee, for we are thine. Into thy hands, Incarnate Saviour, who hast taught us that thou art the way, the truth and the life, receive us and draw us after thee, that we may follow thy steps ; enlighten and guide us, lest the night of sin and error overwhelm us ; abide in us and quicken us by the power of thine indwelling. Into thy hands, O Lord the Spirit, who createst good and destroyest evil, take us and fashion us after thine image : let thy comfort strengthen, thy grace renew, and thy fire cleanse us. Soul and body, in life and in death, in this world of shadows and in thy changeless world of light eternal, now and for ever, Father, Son, and Holy Spirit, into thy hands.

Canon F. B. Macnutt, 1873–1949.

63

FRAGMENTS AND EJACULATIONS

WHEN the Clock strikes, or however else you shall measure the day, it is good to say a short ejaculation every hour, that the parts and returns of devotion may be the measure of your time : and do so also in the breaches of thy sleep ; that those spaces, which have in them no direct business of the world, may be filled with religion.—*Jeremy Taylor*, 1613–1667.

Lord, help my poor soul !—*Edgar Allan Poe*, 1809–1849.

By whose grief our wound was healed : by whose ruin our fall was stayed.—*St. Columban, sixth century, quoted by Dr. Helen Waddell in " Peter Abelard."*

I pray thee, O God, that I may be beautiful within.—*Socrates*, 469–399 B.C.

Oh, Great Spirit, help me never to judge another until I have walked two weeks in his moccasins.—*Sioux Indian prayer.*

And make Thy chosen people joyful.—*Evening Prayer.*

O Lord, help me to remember it is possible to be good in the worst sense.

Lord help me to judge myself by my actions, and other people by their motives.

Glory to God for all things !—*St. Chrysostom, fourth century.*

O wonderful power of Thine ! O glorious virtue ! How much more grace Thou grantest me than e'er I looked for ! —*Benvenuto Cellini*, 1500–1571.

O God! O clemency of Thine, O Virtue infinite! What wonders hast Thou granted me to see this day!— *Cellini.*

Never heed! The Lord's power is over all weakness and death.—*George Fox, 1624–1691.*

Many prayers seem to be unanswered because God has answered them before we prayed.—*Fr. Vincent McNabb.*

God save the phools and don't let them run out, else how can wise men get a livin' ?—*John Billings, U.S.A.*

Oh Lord! that lends me life, Lend me a heart replete with thankfulness!—*II Henry VI, i.I., The King speaking.*

Give him defence against the elements, For I have lost him on a dangerous sea.—*Othello, ii.I., Cassio speaking.*

O Lord, forgive what I have been, sanctify what I am; and order what I shall be.

O give me light to see, a heart to close with and power to do Thy Will, O God.—*Dr. Thomas Wilson, 1663–1755.*

" You make one leetle prayer. You say : 'Le bon Fadder, oh! I want to come back, I so tire, so hungree; so sorree.' "—*A French Canadian, in " Black Rock," by Ralph Connor (Rev. C. W. Gordon, 1860–1937).*

O God, by whom the meek are guided in judgment, grant that the spirit of wisdom may guide me from all false choices, and that walking in Thy straight path I may not stumble or fall.—*William Bright, 1824–1901.*

Save me, O Lord, from the snares of a double mind; deliver me from all cowardly neutralities. Make me to go in the path of Thy commandments, and to trust for my defence in Thy mighty arm alone.—*Richard Hurrell Froude, 1803–1836.*

Guide us in Thy way, O Lord, and mercifully show the fountain of wisdom to our thirsting minds; that we may be free from sorrowful heaviness, and may drink in the sweetness of life eternal.—*Mozarabic.*

The abbot Antony said, " Who sits in solitude and is quiet hath escaped from three wars : hearing, speaking, seeing : yet against one thing shall he continually battle : that is, his own heart."—*Dr. Helen Waddell, in " The Desert Fathers."*

Wilt thou not revive us again, that thy people may rejoice in thee ?—*Psalm lxxxv. 6.*

Be of good courage, and he shall strengthen thine heart : wait, I say, on the Lord.—*Psalm xxvii. 14.*

O God, thou knowest my foolishness ; and my sins are not hid from thee.—*Psalm lxix. 5.*

All that Thou dost ask of us, dear Lord, is that we lend Thee a hand.

Ye shall offer . . . the best thereof, even the hallowed part.—Numbers xviii. 29.

OFFERINGS

TAKE my Christmas
  Let it be
For Thy Crib
  A canopy.

Make my Cross-Day
  Prayers low-said
Pillow for Thy
  Thorn-stabbed Head.

And my Easter
  Carol lie
A carpet for
  Thy Majesty.

Mary Winter Were.

Love is the fulfilling of the law.—Romans xiii. 10.

EASTER

MOST glorious Lord of Lyfe! that, on this day,
Didst make Thy triumph over death and sin;
And, having harrowd hell, didst bring away
Captivity thence captive, us to win:
This joyous day, deare Lord, with joy begin;
And grant that we, for whom thou diddest dye,
Being with Thy deare blood clene washt from sin,
May live for ever in felicity!
And that Thy love we weighing worthily,
May likewise love Thee for the same againe;
And for Thy sake, that all lyke deare didst buy,
With love may one another entertayne!
    So let us love, deare Love, Lyke as we ought,
    Love is the lesson which the Lord us taught.

Edmund Spenser, 1552–1599.

We have a strong city . . . open ye the gates that the righteous nation which keepeth truth may enter in.—
Isaiah xxvi. 1–2.

PRAYER FOR LONDON

LORD, Thou hast made us citizens of a fair city and inheritors of a valiant freedom. Grant that Thy spirit may invest our mightiest endeavours and our humblest toil. Nourish in us the fruits of the spirit that the splendour of London may shine forth in the world, to Thy honour and glory and the welfare of the brethren.

C. H. (*Written for the Mission to London,* 1948).

God the first garden made, and the first city Cain.—
COWLEY.

From LINES IN KENSINGTON GARDENS

CALM soul of all things ! make it mine
To feel, amid the city's jar,
That there abides a peace of thine,
Man did not make, and cannot mar !

The will to neither strive nor cry,
The power to feel with others give !
Calm, calm me more ! nor let me die
Before I have begun to live.

Matthew Arnold, 1822–1888.

DEAR God ! keep him as I knew him, honest and clean and true. . . . Dear God ! if the world is going to spoil him, take him out of the world. Don't let cunning come into his lake-blue eyes. . . . Let him not lose his love of the quiet, healthful things. . . . Don't let him stay too long on the barren flags of London without going where the breath of the mountains gives pride and vigour. . . . Let him keep his courteous demeanour and ceremony. Don't let London and the men of London allure him to put on vulgarity, or the swagger of the cheap gamesters of London. Dear God ! keep him from all evil men."

Jocelyn Dillon, in " The Power of the Dog," by Donn Byrne, 1889–1928.

See whether it be well with thy brethren.—Genesis
xxxvii. 14.

O GOD, Father of the forsaken, the Help of the weak,
the Supplier of the needy; who teachest us that love to-
wards the race of man is the bond of perfectness, and the
imitation of Thy blessed Self; open and touch our hearts,
that we may see and do, both for this world and that which
is to come, the things which belong to our peace.

7th Earl of Shaftesbury, 1801–1885.

BESTOW on me, O Lord, a genial spirit and unwearied
forbearance; a mild, loving, patient heart; kindly looks,
pleasant, cordial speech and manners in the intercourse of
daily life; that I may give offence to none, but as much as
in me lies live in charity with all men.

Johann Arndt, 1555–1621.

O GOD, who of Thy great love to this world, didst reconcile
earth to heaven through Thine Only-Begotten Son; grant
that we, who by the darkness of our sins are turned aside
from brotherly love, may by Thy light shed forth in our
souls Thine own sweetness and embrace our friends in Thee,
forgiving our enemies, even as Thou, for Thy Son's sake,
dost forgive us.

Mozarabic.

To shew forth thy loving-kindness in the morning, and thy faithfulness every night.—Psalm xcii. 2.

BE pleased, O Lord, to remember my friends, all that have prayed for me, and all that have done me good.

Do Thou good to them and return all their kindness double into their own bosom, rewarding them with blessings, and sanctifying them with Thy graces, and bringing them to glory. . . .

Let all my family and kindred, my neighbours and acquaintance receive the benefit of my prayers, and the blessings of God; the comforts and supports of Thy providence, and the sanctification of Thy Spirit.

Jeremy Taylor, 1613–1667.

Friendship, of itself a holy tie.—DRYDEN.

O GOD, our heavenly Father, who hast commanded us to love one another as Thy children, and has ordained the highest friendship in the bond of Thy Spirit, we beseech Thee to maintain and preserve us always in the same bond, to Thy glory, and our mutual comfort, with all those to whom we are bound by any special tie, either of nature or of choice; that we may be perfected together in that love which is from above, and which never faileth when all other things shall fail.

Send down the dew of Thy heavenly grace upon us, that we may have joy in each other that passeth not away; and having lived together in love here, according to Thy commandment, may live for ever together with them, being made one in Thee, in Thy glorious kingdom hereafter, through Jesus Christ, Our Lord.

George Hickes, 1642–1715.

POUR on us, O Lord, the spirit of love and brotherly-kindness; so that, sprinkled by the dew of Thy benediction, we may be made glad by Thy glory and grace; through Christ our Lord.

Sarum Breviary.

By the which will we are sanctified.—Hebrews x. 10.

A LOVER'S PRAYER

O GOD of earth and heaven,
And the waters that cover the sea;
Bestow on us Thy leaven,
And give my love to me.

T. T.

A mind content both crown and kingdom is.—GREENE.

GIVE me, O Lord, a tender conscience; a conversation discreet and affable, modest and patient, liberal and obliging; a body chaste and healthful, competency of living according to my condition, contentedness in all estates, a resigned will and mortified affections: that I may be as Thou wouldest have me, and my portion may be in the lot of the righteous, in the brightness of Thy countenance, and the glories of eternity.

Jeremy Taylor, 1613–1667.

O ALMIGHTY God, eternal treasure of all good things, never let my desires of this world be greedy, nor my thoughts intemperate, nor my cares vexatious and distracting; but moderate, holy, subordinate to Thy will, the measure Thou hast appointed me.

Jeremy Taylor, 1613–1667.

O GOD, Who has chosen the weak things of the world to confound the mighty, do Thou shed forth continual day upon us who watch for Thee; that our lips may praise Thee, our life may bless Thee, and our meditations glorify Thee.

Sarum Breviary.

Let this child's soul come into him again.—I Kings xvii. 21.

MAKER of me, go on making me, and let me help Thee. Come, oh Father, here I am : let us go on. I know that my words are those of a child, but it is Thy child that prays to Thee. It is Thy dark I walk in, it is Thy hand I hold.

George MacDonald, 1824–1905, in " Castle Warlock."

In my Father's house are many mansions.—John xiv. 2.

ST. NICHOLAS

WILL you, Father Nicholas,
Sometimes pray for me?
Will you give me too a place
In your family?
Boys and girls and sailormen
And pawnbrokers are there:
Will you, Father Nicholas,
Grant me too a share?
Then, please God, you'll lead us all
Up into His heavenly Hall.

B. C. Boulter.

That which was written was upright, even words of truth.—Ecclesiastes xii. 10.

PRAYER FOR RICHARD

RICHARD, run ryghte
In Life's race :
Christ thy myghte,
His thy grace ;
His thy lyghte
Round thy wayes
All thy dayes.

*B. C. Boulter : for the baptism of Richard Southby, grandson of
Lady Southby.*

Thou wilt shew me the path of life : in thy presence is fulness of joy.—Psalm xvi. 11.

PRAYER FOR JAMES

SAINT JAMES THE LESS,

We pray thee, bless

Young James' childhood days :

And, prithee, later

Saint James the Greater,

Conduct him through life's tortuous ways :

Then, less and greater, he shall bring

Smiles for our frowns, hope for our suffering.

B. C. Boulter : lines written for the baptism of James Piercy,
grandson of Lord Piercy.

For such a child I blesse God, in whose bosom he is! May I and mine become as this little child.—EVELYN.

GIVE, I pray Thee, to all children grace reverently to love their parents, and lovingly to obey them. Teach us all that filial duty never ends or lessens; and bless all parents in their children, and all children in their parents.

O Thou in whom the fatherless find mercy, make all orphans, I beseech Thee, loving and dutiful unto Thee, their true Father. Be Thy will their law, Thy house their home, Thy love their inheritance.

And I earnestly pray Thee, comfort those who have lost their children, giving mothers grace to be comforted though they are not; and grant us all faith to yield our dearest treasures unto Thee with joy and thanksgiving, that where with Thee our treasure is, there our hearts may be also. Thus may we look for and hasten unto the day of union with Thee, and of reunion.

Christina Rossetti, 1830–1894.

BLESS my children with healthful bodies, with good understandings, with the graces and gifts of Thy Spirit, with sweet dispositions and holy habits, and sanctify them throughout in their bodies and Souls and spirits, and keep them unblameable to the coming of the Lord Jesus.

Jeremy Taylor, 1613–1667.

For this child I prayed. . . .—I Samuel i. 27.

OUR LADY OF DORMITORIES
(First day of term)

O MARY, look upon my son ;
Though brave his heart and bright,
His tale of years but numbers eight—
Alone at school tonight.

Comfort and strengthen his small soul,
And if he needs must cry,
Sweet Mary, grant it may not be
When other boys are by.

Brood o'er him with thy tenderness
That so he may not miss
Too much the cosy tucking-up,
The laughing good-night kiss.

Keep him from loneliness and fear ;
Guard thou his thoughts from ill :
So shall he know, though far from me,
A Mother's presence still.

Teresa Hooley.

AN ATHLETE'S PRAYER

HELP me to play the game, dear Lord,
   With all my might and main;
Grant me the courage born of right.
   A heart to stand the strain.

Send me a sense of humour, Lord,
   To laugh when victory's mine—
To laugh, if I should meet defeat,
   Without a fret or whine.

Give me the grace to follow rules,
   Confess when I am wrong,
When silence or the other thing
   Wins plaudits from the throng.

When foes are tough and fighting fierce
   And I am getting weak,
Dear God, don't ever let me show
   A broad, bright yellow streak.

And teach me, Lord, life's game to play
   Just one day at a time—
With Thee as coach and trainer, Lord,
   Real victory must be mine.

Rev. Frederick D. Tyner.

Now the God of hope fill you with all joy and peace in believing, that ye may abound in hope. . . .—Romans xv. 13.

From PRAYER FOR A BLESSING

BESTOW, dear Lord, upon our youth
  The gift of saving grace;
And let the seed of sacred truth
  Fall in a fruitful place.

We pray that you may early prove
  The Spirit's power to teach;
You cannot be too young to love
  That Jesus whom we preach.

William Cowper, 1731–1800.

PRAYER

GRANT me, O Lord,
When the days come that I am grey and tired,
Ne'er to grow bitter of heart, ne'er to forget
I, too, have loved and longed and been desired.

Lest, one sad hour,
Should come my son, of that past love begotten,
Seeking for understanding, and should say
" She is too old, too old.   She has forgotten."

Teresa Hooley.

The fear of the Lord, that is wisdom.—Job xxviii. 28.

ALMIGHTY God, the giver of wisdom, without whose help resolutions are vain, without whose blessing study is ineffectual; enable me, if it be Thy will, to attain such knowledge as may qualify me to direct the doubtful, and instruct the ignorant; to prevent wrongs and terminate contentions; and grant that I may use that knowledge which I shall attain, to Thy glory and my own salvation, for Jesus Christ's sake.

Dr. Samuel Johnson, 1709–1784.

I will not keep silence, but will recompense.—Isaiah lxv. 6.

THE UNKIND SILENCE

O LORD give me strength to refrain from the unkind silence that is born of hardness of heart; the unkind silence that clouds the serenity of understanding and is the enemy of peace.

Give me strength to be the first to tender the healing word and the renewal of friendship, that the bonds of amity and the flow of charity may be strengthened for the good of the brethren and the furthering of Thine eternal, loving purpose.

C. H.

Yet in my walks it seems to me That the Grace of God is in Courtesy.—BELLOC.

O ALMIGHTY God, give to Thy servant a meek and gentle spirit, that I may be slow to anger, and easy to mercy and forgiveness.

Give me a wise and constant heart, that I may never be moved to an intemperate anger for any injury that is done or offered.

Lord, let me ever be courteous, and easy to be entreated; let me never fall into a peevish or contentious spirit, but follow peace with all men; offering forgiveness, inviting them by courtesies, ready to confess my own errors, apt to make amends, and desirous to be reconciled.

Let no sickness or cross accident, no employment or weariness, make me angry or ungentle and discontented, or unthankful, or uneasy to them that minister to me; but in all things make me like unto the holy Jesus.

Jeremy Taylor, 1613–1667.

For the fruit of the Spirit is in all goodness and righteousness and truth.—Ephesians v. 9.

LET thy law, Almighty! be the rule, and Thy glory the constant end of all I do! Let me not build virtue on any notions of honour, but of honour to Thy name. Let me not sink piety in the boast of benevolence; my love of God in the love of my fellow-creatures. Can good be of human growth! No! It is Thy gift, Almighty, and All-good! Let not Thy bounties remove the Donor from my thought; nor the love of pleasures make me forsake the Fountain from which they flow. When joys entice, let me ask their title to my heart. When evils threaten, let me see Thy mercy shining through the cloud; and discern the great hazard of having all to my wish. In an age of such licence, let me not take comfort from an inauspicious omen, the number of those who do amiss; an omen rather of public ruin, than of private safety. Let the joys of the multitude less allure than alarm me; and their danger, not example, determine my choice. What, weight public example, passion, and the multitude, in one scale, against reason, and the Almighty, in the other?

In this day of domineering pleasure, so lower my taste, as to make me relish the comforts of life. And in this day of dissipation, O give me thought sufficient to preserve me from being so desperate, as in this perpetual flux of things, to depend on to-morrow: a dependence that is the ruin of to-day; as that is of eternity. Let my whole existence be ever before me: nor let the terrors of the grave turn back my survey. When temptations arise, and virtue staggers, let imagination sound the final trumpet, and judgment lay hold on eternal life. In what is well begun, grant me to persevere; and to know, that none are wise, but they who determine to be wiser still.

And since, O Lord! the fear of Thee is the beginning of wisdom; and, in its progress, its surest shield, turn the world entirely out of my heart, and place that guardian angel, Thy blessed fear, in its stead. Turn out a foolish world, which gives its money for what is not bread; which hews out broken cisterns that hold no water: a world in which even they, whose hands are mighty, have found nothing. There *is* nothing, Lord God Almighty, in heaven, in earth, but Thee. I will seek Thy face, bless Thy name, sing Thy praises, love Thy law, do Thy will, enjoy Thy peace, hope Thy glory, till my final hour! Thus shall I grasp all that can be grasped by man. This will heighten good, and soften evil, in the present life! And when Death summons, I shall sleep sweetly in the dust, till his mighty Conqueror bids the trumpet sound; and then shall I, through His merits, awake to eternal glory.

Prayer of Sir Charles Grandison, in the novel of that name by Samuel Richardson, 1689–1761.

I believed, therefore have I spoken: I was greatly afflicted . . . I will pay my vows unto the Lord now in the presence of all his people.—Psalm cxvi. 10–19.

PRAYER IN LEAN DAYS

De Profundis, here burn I
Candles to Saint Anthony—
Patron saint of treasures lost,
World-precious and transcending cost.
Give back our heritage of wonder
For things around us, over, under
(Seed in the womb and in the earth,
Growing through darkness up to birth);
Give back, for healing, present laughter,
Though terror gloom before and after
(Potent the stream of humour runs
To cleanse the soul from taint of guns).
Restore the spark within the clod,
Give back belief in Man—and God.

Teresa Hooley.

A merry heart maketh a cheerful countenance.—Proverbs
XV. 13.

O GOD, animate us to cheerfulness. May we have a joyful sense of our blessings, learn to look on the bright circumstances of our lot, and maintain a perpetual contentedness. Preserve us from despondency and from yielding to dejection. Teach us that nothing can hurt us if, with true loyalty of affection, we keep Thy commandments and take refuge in Thee.

William E. Channing, 1780–1842.

Magnify him with thanksgiving.—Psalm lxix. 30.

A THANKSGIVING

WE thank Thee for Thy tender love
　　And for Thy sheltering care ;
For shadows lifted, ways made plain,
　　Joyousness everywhere.

We thank Thee, too, for strength received
　　To face life day by day ;
For health and beauty, love and joy,
　　And all that makes life gay.

We thank Thee every waking morn,
　　And every sleeping eve ;
For countless blessings day by day,
　　Dear Lord, our thanks receive.

　　　　　　　　　　Margaret H. Hancock.

It is the gift of God.—Ecclesiastes iii. 13.

TWO GIFTS

WE thank Thee, Lord, for Memory
  To live again the past ;
That in remembering bygone days
  The fruits of joy shall last.

But for the power to forget
  We thank Thee even more :
The stings, the slights, the hurts, the wounds,
  Can never hurt us more.

Margaret H. Hancock.

O day most calm, most bright, The fruit of this, the next world's bud.—HERBERT.

" THE Sunday before his death, he rose suddenly from his Bed or Couch, call'd for one of his Instruments, took it into hand, and said—

> My God, My God,
> My Musick shall find thee,
>> And every string
> shall have his attribute to sing.

And having tun'd it, he play'd and sung :

> The Sundays of Mans life,
> Thredded together on times string,
> Make Bracelets, to adorn the Wife
> Of the eternal glorious King :
> On Sundays, Heavens dore stands ope ;
> Blessings are plentiful and rife,
>> More plentiful than hope.

Izaak Walton, 1593–1683, in " *The Life of George Herbert.*"

And from the hills I behold him.—Numbers xxiii. 9.

Give me a free heart
Since upon the everlasting hills I have set my gaze ;
And through those hills my feet shall seek Thy ways,
And I shall start
The race toward that vast
Beatitude, the essential sight of Thee,
Nor rest till on the horizon of Eternity
I'll find Thee at the last.

Mary Winter Were.

Eternal Goodness, who givest loveliness to the earth, and gladness to the heart ; we worship Thee. We praise Thee for the wonderful life of summer ; for the beauty spread upon the hills, and for the flowers that fill the valley with sweetness. Oh Life that breathest in all fair and sweet things, quicken us ! Spirit of beauty, dwell in us !

(?) *Dr. John Hunter.*

Giving thanks always for all things.—Ephesians v. 20.

O LORD my God, for life and reason, nurture, preservation, guidance, education; for Thy gifts of grace and nature, for Thy calling, recalling, manifold recalling me again; for Thy forbearance, long-suffering, and long long-suffering toward me, even until now; for all from who I have received any good or help; for the use of Thy present good things; for Thy promise, and my hope, of good things to come; for all these things, and for all other, which I know, which I know not, manifest or secret, remembered or forgotten by me, I praise Thee, I bless Thee, I give Thee thanks; and I will praise, and bless, and give Thee thanks, all the days of my life.

What shall I render unto the Lord for all His benefits to me? Thou art worthy, O Lord, to receive glory, and honour, and power.

Lancelot Andrewes, 1555–1626.

God created . . . every living creature . . . and saw that it was good.—Genesis 1. 21.

O GOD, my Master, should I gain the grace
    To see Thee face to face when life is ended,
    Grant that a little dog, who once pretended
That I was God, may see me face to face!

B. C. Boulter, from the French of Francis Jammes.

I PRAY thee, Lord, the Father, and the Guide of our reason, that we may remember the nobleness with which Thou hast adorned us ; and that Thou would'st be always on our right hand and on our left, in the motion of our own wills ; that so we may be purged from the contagion of the body and the affections of the brute, and overcome them and rule, and use, as it becomes men to use them, for instruments. And then that Thou would'st be in Fellowship with us for the careful correction of our reason, and for the conjunction by the light of truth with the things that truly are.

And in the third place, I pray Thee the Saviour, that Thou would'st utterly cleanse away the closing gloom from the eyes of our souls, that we may know well who is to be held for God, and who for mortal.

Last prayer of George Chapman, 1559–1634.

Redeeming the time, because the days are evil.—
Ephesians v. 16.

O ETERNAL God, who hast created me to do the work of God after the manner of men, give me Thy grace that I may be a prudent spender of my time, so that I may be profitable to the Christian commonwealth; and by discharging all my duty, may glorify Thee.

Jeremy Taylor, 1613–1667.

O LORD, renew our spirits that our work may not be to us a burden, but a delight. Oh, let us not serve Thee with the spirit of bondage as slaves, but with the cheerfulness and gladness of children, delighting ourselves in Thee, and rejoicing in Thy work.

Benjamin Jenks, 1646–1724.

And, having done all, to stand.—Ephesians vi. 13.

O GOD our Father, let us not be content to wait and see what will happen, but give us the determination to make the right things happen.

While time is running out, save us from patience which is akin to cowardice.

Give us the courage to be either hot or cold, to stand for something, lest we fall for anything. In Jesus' name, Amen.

Dr. Peter Marshall (1902–1949), *Chaplain to U.S. Congress.*
Used in the Senate, March 10, 1948.

*And . . . giving all diligence, add to your faith virtue ;
and to virtue knowledge.*—II Peter i. 5.

A PRAYER TO BE SAID BY MERCHANTS, TRADESMEN, AND HANDICRAFTS-MEN.

O ETERNAL God, Thou Fountain of justice, mercy and benediction, who by my education and other effects of Thy Providence hast called me to this profession, that by my industry I may in my small proportion work together for the good of myself and others : I humbly beg Thy grace to guide me in my intention, and in the transaction of my affairs, so that I may be diligent, just, and faithful ; and give me Thy favour, that this my labour may be accepted by Thee as part of my necessary duty : and give me Thy blessing to assist and prosper me in my calling, to such measures as Thou shalt in mercy choose for me : and be pleased to let Thy Holy Spirit be for ever present with me, that I may never be given to covetousness and sordid appetites, to lying and falsehood, or any other base, indirect and beggarly arts ; but give me prudence, honesty, and Christian sincerity, that my Trade may be sanctified by my Religion, my labour by my intention and Thy blessing ; that, when I have done my portion of work Thou hast allotted me, and improved the talent Thou hast intrusted to me, and served the Common-wealth in my capacity, I may receive the mighty price of my high calling, which I expect and beg, in the portion and inheritance of the ever-blessed Saviour and Redeemer Jesus.

Jeremy Taylor, 1613–1667.

Where there is no vision, the people perish ; but he that keepeth the law, happy is he.—Proverbs xxix. 18.

O God, keep me on the path of achieving happiness and success that are real. Keep my vision always clear to see the goals. Help me to tap the hidden powers within and above me. Give me strength to work with all the energies of mind and body. Help me to practise the love of people and service to others. Keep me forever with a smile on my face for the whole human race.

Henry J. Kaiser.

God shall supply all your need, according to his riches in glory.—Philippians iv. 19.

From ANDREW RYKMAN'S PRAYER

PARDON, Lord, the lips that dare
Shape in words a mortal's prayer!
Prayer that, when my day is done,
And I see the setting sun,
Shorn and beamless, cold and dim,
Sink beneath the horizon's rim—
When this ball of rock and clay
Crumbles from my feet away,
And the solid shores and sense
Melt into the vague immense,
Father! I may come to Thee,
Even with the beggar's plea,
As the poorest of Thy poor,
With my needs, and nothing more. . . .

Thus did Andrew Rykman pray,
Are we wiser, better grown,
That we may not, in our day,
Make his prayer our own?

John Greenleaf Whittier, 1807–1892.

In him was life; and the life was the light of men.—
John i. 4.

PRAYER FOR THE NIGHT

FOUNTAIN of light. Light, Source of Light,
    Hear our prayer.
Our dark sins put to flight,
    O seek us, kindly Light.

Whose holy strength created man,
    Whose law condemned, whose love redeemed,
Be Thou in all men Love and Law
    Omnipotent.

The labour of the day is done,
    And we are safe,
Beneath the covert of Thy shield
    We give Thee praise.

The sun hath left us, comes the dark,
    Shine forth, O Sun.
Whose light is golden on the face
    Of the angel host.

Pour down Thy radiant light
    On our dim clouded mind.
Kindle us with Thy touch
    That we may burn.

From horror, lust and fear,
    Guard Thou our sleep,
And if we sleep not, may our eyes behold
    The citizens of God.

Alcuin, 735–804, translated by Dr. Helen Waddell.

I will both lay me down in peace, and sleep.—Psalm iv. 8.

ALMIGHTY and Everlasting God, Who commandest Thy mercy in the day time, and in the night season declarest the same: We humbly beseech Thee, Who hast preserved us this day in safety, that tonight Thou wilt guard our rest; through Jesus Christ our Lord.

Mozarabic.

CLOSE now thine eyes, and rest secure;
 Thy soul is safe enough, thy body sure;
  He that loves thee, He that keeps
And guards thee, never slumbers, never sleeps.
The smiling Conscience in a sleeping breast
 Has only peace, has only rest:
  The music and the mirth of kings
Are all but discords, when she sings;
 Then close thine eyes and rest secure;
No sleep so sweet as thine, no rest so sure.

Francis Quarles, 1592–1644.

And meditate on thee in the night watches.—Psalm lxiii. 6.

O LORD God and heavenly Father, which according to Thy manifold wisdom, hast appointed the day for labour, and the night for rest; we render Thee thanks, that thou has so mercifully kept us this day, and hast heaped continually upon us so many benefits.

Grant likewise, that we now ceasing from our labour and care, may so be refreshed with sleep, that our minds not being buried in sleep with the body, we be slumbering in Thy love; but that the memory of our creation and salvation, be at no time wiped out of our hearts.

Grant, moreover, that our consciences, as well as our bodies, may enjoy Thy own rest. Likewise, that we moderately using sleep, we may have a respect, not unto sluggishness, but to necessity, to the end that we returning more apt and quick to our works, left off for a time, we may the more readily serve thee and profit our neighbour: And in the mean time, while we are taking rest, deliver us from all peril . . .

We beseech Thee, that as the night now foldeth us all things in darkness, so according to thy incomprehensible mercy, that Thou wilt bury all our sins, lest for them we be casten out from Thy sight.

Grant also quietness and comfort to all those which are afflicted with any kind of sickness, or other calamities, for Christ Jesus Thy Son our Lord's sake, which this way hath taught us to pray, Our Father which art in Heaven. . . .

The Scottish Catechism.

Through the thanksgiving of many, redound to the glory of God.—II Corinthians iv. 15.

LORD, with what courage and delight
  I do each thing,
When Thy least breath sustains my wing!
  I shine and move
  Like those above,
  And, with much gladness
  Quitting sadness,
Make me fair days of every night.

Affliction thus mere pleasure is;
  And hap what will,
If Thou be in't, 'tis welcome still.
  But since Thy rays
  In sunny days
  Thou dost thus lend
  And freely spend,
Ah! what shall I return for this.

O that I were all soul! that Thou
  Wouldst make each part
Of this poor, sinful frame, pure heart!
  Then would I drown
  My single one
  And to Thy praise
  A consort raise
Of hallelujahs here below.

Henry Vaughan, 1622–1695.

HE prayeth best, who loveth best
All things both great and small;

For the dear God who loveth us,
He made and loveth all.

Samuel Taylor Coleridge, 1772–1834.

FINALLY, brethren, whatsoever things are true, whatsoever things are honest, whatsoever things are just, whatsoever things are pure, whatsoever things are lovely, whatsoever things are of good report; if there be any virtue, and if there be any praise, think on these things.

Those things which ye have both learned, and received and heard, and seen in me, do : and the God of peace shall be with you.

Philippians, iv. 8–9.

INDEX

INDEX OF FIRST LINES

114

FOR PERSONAL ADDITIONS

FOR PERSONAL ADDITIONS

FOR PERSONAL ADDITIONS

FOR PERSONAL ADDITIONS

FOR PERSONAL ADDITIONS

FOR PERSONAL ADDITIONS

FOR PERSONAL ADDITIONS

FOR PERSONAL ADDITIONS

FOR PERSONAL ADDITIONS

FOR PERSONAL ADDITIONS

FOR PERSONAL ADDITIONS

FOR PERSONAL ADDITIONS